HERSHEY'S ®

Sweet Treats & More

Favorite cookies, brownies, and bites

Publications International, Ltd.

Microwave Cooking: Microwave ovens vary in wattage. Use the cooking times as guidelines and check for doneness before adding more time.

Table of Contents

Classic Favorites

Rich Dark Tiger Cookies

Makes about 4 dozen cookies

1½ cups granulated sugar

½ cup vegetable oil

½ cup HERSHEY'S SPECIAL DARK Cocoa or HERSHEY'S Cocoa

3 eggs

1½ teaspoons vanilla extract

1¾ cups all-purpose flour

1½ teaspoons baking powder

½ teaspoon salt

Powdered sugar

48 HERSHEY'S KISSESBRAND SPECIAL DARK Mildly Sweet Chocolates or HERSHEY'S KISSESBRAND Milk Chocolates, unwrapped (optional)

1. Stir together granulated sugar and oil in large bowl; add cocoa, beating until well blended. Beat in eggs and vanilla. Stir together flour, baking powder and salt; gradually add to cocoa mixture, beating well.

2. Cover; refrigerate until dough is firm enough to handle, at least 6 hours.

3. Heat oven to 350°F. Grease cookie sheet or line with parchment paper. Shape dough into 1-inch balls (dough will still be sticky); roll in powdered sugar to coat. Place about 2 inches apart on prepared cookie sheet.

4. Bake 11 to 13 minutes or until almost no indentation remains when touched lightly and tops are cracked. Immediately press chocolate piece into center of each cookie, if desired. Cool slightly. Transfer to wire rack. Cool completely.

Best Fudgey Pecan Brownies

Makes about 16 brownies

½ **cup (1 stick) butter or margarine,
   melted**

1 **cup sugar**

1 **teaspoon vanilla extract**

2 **eggs**

½ **cup all-purpose flour**

⅓ **cup HERSHEY'S Cocoa**

¼ **teaspoon baking powder**

¼ **teaspoon salt**

½ **cup coarsely chopped pecans**

   **CHOCOLATE PECAN FROSTING
   (recipe follows)**

   Pecan halves

1. Heat oven to 350°F. Lightly grease 8- or 9-inch square baking pan.

2. Beat butter, sugar and vanilla with spoon in large bowl. Add eggs; beat well. Stir together flour, cocoa, baking powder and salt; gradually add to egg mixture, beating until well blended. Stir in chopped pecans. Spread in prepared pan.

3. Bake 20 to 25 minutes or until brownies begin to pull away from sides of pan. Meanwhile, prepare CHOCOLATE PECAN FROSTING. Spread warm frosting over warm brownies. Garnish with pecan halves. Cool completely; cut into squares.

Chocolate Pecan Frosting

Makes about 1 cup frosting

1⅓ cups powdered sugar
2 tablespoons HERSHEY'S Cocoa
3 tablespoons butter or margarine
2 tablespoons milk
¼ teaspoon vanilla extract
¼ cup chopped pecans

1. Stir together powdered sugar and cocoa in medium bowl.

2. Heat butter and milk in small saucepan over low heat until butter is melted. Gradually beat into cocoa mixture, beating until smooth. Stir in vanilla and pecans.

REESE'S® Peanut Butter Bark

Makes about 1 pound candy

2   packages (4 ounces each) HERSHEY'S Semi-Sweet Chocolate Baking Bars, broken into pieces

1⅔ cups (10-ounce package) REESE'S Peanut Butter Chips

1   tablespoon shortening (do not use butter, margarine, spread or oil)

½   cup roasted peanuts or toasted almonds,* coarsely chopped

To toast almonds: Heat oven to 350°F. Spread almonds in thin layer in shallow baking pan. Bake 8 to 10 minutes, stirring occasionally, until light golden brown; cool.

1. Cover tray with wax paper.

2. Place chocolate in medium microwave-safe bowl. Microwave at MEDIUM (50%) 1 minute; stir. If necessary, microwave at MEDIUM an additional 15 seconds at a time, stirring after each heating, until chocolate is melted and smooth when stirred.

3. Immediately place peanut butter chips and shortening in second microwave-safe bowl. Microwave at MEDIUM 1 minute; stir. If necessary, microwave at MEDIUM an additional 15 seconds at a time, stirring after each heating, until chips are melted and mixture is smooth when stirred; stir in peanuts.

4. Alternately spoon above mixtures onto prepared tray; swirl with knife for marbled effect. Gently tap tray on countertop to even thickness of mixture. Cover; refrigerate until firm. Break into pieces. Store in cool, dry place.

HERSHEY'S® Rich Cocoa Fudge

Makes about 3 dozen pieces or 1¾ pounds candy

3 **cups sugar**

⅔ **cup HERSHEY'S Cocoa or HERSHEY'S SPECIAL DARK Cocoa**

⅛ **teaspoon salt**

1½ **cups milk**

¼ **cup (½ stick) butter**

1 **teaspoon vanilla extract**

1. Line 8- or 9-inch square pan with foil, extending foil over edges of pan. Butter foil.

2. Stir together sugar, cocoa and salt in heavy 4-quart saucepan; stir in milk. Cook over medium heat, stirring constantly, until mixture comes to full rolling boil. Boil, without stirring, until mixture reaches 234°F on candy thermometer or until small amount of mixture dropped into very cold water forms a soft ball which flattens when removed from water. (Bulb of candy thermometer should not rest on bottom of saucepan.) Remove from heat.

3. Add butter and vanilla. DO NOT STIR. Cool at room temperature to 110°F (lukewarm). Beat with wooden spoon until fudge thickens and just begins to lose some of its gloss (about 7 minutes). Quickly spread in prepared pan; cool completely. Cut into squares. Store in tightly covered container at room temperature.

Nutty Rich Cocoa Fudge: Beat cooked fudge as directed. Immediately stir in 1 cup chopped almonds, pecans or walnuts and quickly spread in prepared pan.

Marshmallow Nut Cocoa Fudge: Increase cocoa to ¾ cup. Cook fudge as directed. Add 1 cup marshmallow creme with butter and vanilla. DO NOT STIR. Cool to 110°F (lukewarm). Beat 8 minutes; stir in 1 cup chopped nuts. Pour into prepared pan. (Fudge does not set until poured into pan.)

Notes:
For best results, do not double this recipe.
This is one of our most requested recipes, but also one of our most difficult. The directions
must be followed exactly. Beat too little and the fudge is too soft. Beat too long and it
becomes hard and sugary.

11 | Classic Favorites

Chocolate Seven Layer Bars

Makes about 24 bars

1½ cups finely crushed thin pretzels or pretzel sticks

¾ cup (1½ sticks) butter or margarine, melted

1 can (14 ounces) sweetened condensed milk (not evaporated milk)

1 package (4 ounces) HERSHEY'S Unsweetened Chocolate Baking Bar, broken into pieces

2 cups miniature marshmallows

1 cup MOUNDS Sweetened Coconut Flakes

1 cup coarsely chopped pecans

1 package (4 ounces) HERSHEY'S Semi-Sweet Chocolate Baking Bar, broken into pieces

1 tablespoon shortening (do not use butter, margarine, spread or oil)

1. Heat oven to 350°F. Combine pretzels and melted butter in small bowl; press evenly onto bottom of ungreased 13×9×2-inch baking pan.

2. Place sweetened condensed milk and unsweetened chocolate in small microwave-safe bowl. Microwave at MEDIUM (50%) 1 minute; stir. If necessary, microwave at MEDIUM an additional 15 seconds at a time, stirring after each heating, until mixture is melted and smooth when stirred. Carefully pour over pretzel layer in pan. Top with marshmallows, coconut and pecans; press firmly down onto chocolate layer.

3. Bake 25 to 30 minutes or until lightly browned; cool completely in pan on wire rack.

4. Melt semi-sweet chocolate and shortening in small microwave-safe bowl at MEDIUM (50%) 1 minute or until melted when stirred; drizzle over entire top. Refrigerate 15 minutes or until glaze is set. Cut into bars.

HERSHEY'S® All American HEATH® Brownies

Makes 16 brownies

⅓ cup butter or margarine

3 sections (½ ounce each) HERSHEY'S Unsweetened Chocolate Baking Bar

1 cup sugar

2 eggs

1 teaspoon vanilla extract

1 cup all-purpose flour

½ teaspoon baking powder

¼ teaspoon salt

1⅓ cups (8-ounce package) HEATH Milk Chocolate Toffee Bits

1. Heat oven to 350°F. Grease bottom of 8-inch square baking pan.

2. Melt butter and chocolate in medium saucepan over low heat, stirring occasionally. Stir in sugar. Add eggs, one at a time, beating after each addition. Stir in vanilla. Combine flour, baking powder and salt; add to chocolate mixture, stirring until well blended. Spread batter in prepared pan.

3. Bake 20 minutes or until brownie begins to pull away from sides of pan. Remove from oven; sprinkle with toffee bits. Cover tightly with foil and cool completely on wire rack. Remove foil; cut into squares.

Peanut Butter Blossoms

Makes about 4 dozen cookies

48 **HERSHEY'S KISSES**BRAND **Milk Chocolates**

¾ **cup REESE'S Creamy Peanut Butter**

½ **cup shortening**

⅓ **cup granulated sugar**

⅓ **cup packed light brown sugar**

1 **egg**

2 **tablespoons milk**

1 **teaspoon vanilla extract**

1½ **cups all-purpose flour**

1 **teaspoon baking soda**

½ **teaspoon salt**

Additional granulated sugar

1. Heat oven to 375°F. Remove wrappers from chocolates.

2. Beat peanut butter and shortening with electric mixer on medium speed in large bowl until well blended. Add ⅓ cup granulated sugar and brown sugar; beat until fluffy. Add egg, milk and vanilla; beat well. Stir together flour, baking soda and salt; gradually beat into peanut butter mixture.

3. Shape dough into 1-inch balls. Roll in additional granulated sugar; place on ungreased cookie sheet.

4. Bake 8 to 10 minutes or until lightly browned. Immediately press a chocolate into center of each cookie; cookies will crack around edges. Remove to wire racks and cool completely.

Peanut Butter and Milk Chocolate Chip Brownie Bars

Makes about 24 bars

6 tablespoons butter or margarine, melted

1¼ cups sugar

2 teaspoons vanilla extract, divided

3 eggs

1 cup plus 2 tablespoons all-purpose flour

⅓ cup HERSHEY'S Cocoa

½ teaspoon baking powder

½ teaspoon salt

1 can (14 ounces) sweetened condensed milk (not evaporated milk)

½ cup REESE'S Creamy Peanut Butter

1 cup HERSHEY'S Milk Chocolate Chips, divided

1 cup REESE'S Peanut Butter Chips, divided

¾ teaspoon shortening

1. Heat oven to 350°F. Grease 13×9×2-inch baking pan. Stir together butter, sugar and 1 teaspoon vanilla in large bowl. Add 2 eggs; stir until blended. Stir together flour, cocoa, baking powder and salt. Add to egg mixture, stirring until blended. Spread in prepared pan. Bake 20 minutes.

2. Meanwhile, stir together sweetened condensed milk, peanut butter, remaining egg and remaining 1 teaspoon vanilla extract. Pour evenly over hot brownie. Set aside 1 tablespoon each milk chocolate chips and peanut butter chips; sprinkle remaining chips over peanut butter mixture. Return to oven; continue baking 20 to 25 minutes or until peanut butter layer is set and edges begin to brown. Cool completely in pan on wire rack.

3. Stir together remaining milk chocolate chips, remaining peanut butter chips and shortening in small microwave-safe bowl. Microwave at MEDIUM (50%) 30 seconds; stir. If necessary, microwave at MEDIUM an additional 15 seconds at a time, stirring after each heating, until chips are melted and mixture is smooth when stirred. Drizzle over top of bars. When drizzle is firm, cut into bars. Store loosely covered at room temperature.

HERSHEY'S® Giant Chocolate Chip Cookie

Makes 10 servings

6 tablespoons (¾ stick) butter or margarine, softened

½ cup granulated sugar

¼ cup packed light brown sugar

½ teaspoon vanilla extract

1 egg

1 cup all-purpose flour

½ teaspoon baking soda

1⅔ cups HERSHEY'S SPECIAL DARK Chocolate Chips, HERSHEY'S Semi-Sweet Chocolate Chips, HERSHEY'S Mini Chips Semi-Sweet Chocolate or HERSHEY'S Milk Chocolate Chips

1. Heat oven to 350°F. Line 12-inch metal pizza pan with foil.

2. Beat butter, granulated sugar, brown sugar and vanilla in medium bowl until fluffy; add egg, beating well. Stir together flour and baking soda; stir into mixture with chocolate chips. Spread batter evenly in prepared pan, spreading to 1-inch from edge.

3. Bake 18 to 22 minutes or until lightly brown and set. Cool completely; carefully lift cookie from pan and remove foil. Decorate as desired; cut into wedges to serve.

"Perfectly Chocolate" Giant Chocolate Chip Cookie: Stir in ⅓ cup HERSHEY'S Cocoa or HERSHEY'S SPECIAL DARK Cocoa with flour mixture.

Chippy Chewy Bars

Makes 24 bars

½ cup (1 stick) butter or margarine

1½ cups graham cracker crumbs

1⅔ cups (10-ounce package) REESE'S Peanut Butter Chips

1½ cups MOUNDS Sweetened Coconut Flakes

1 can (14 ounces) sweetened condensed milk (not evaporated milk)

½ cup HERSHEY'S SPECIAL DARK Chocolate Chips, HERSHEY'S Semi-Sweet Chocolate Chips or HERSHEY'S Mini Chips Semi-Sweet Chocolate

¾ teaspoon shortening (do not use butter, margarine, spread or oil)

1. Heat oven to 350°F. Place butter in 13×9×2-inch baking pan. Heat in oven until melted; remove pan from oven. Sprinkle graham cracker crumbs evenly over butter; press down with fork.

2. Sprinkle peanut butter chips over crumbs; sprinkle coconut over chips. Drizzle sweetened condensed milk evenly over top.

3. Bake 20 minutes or until lightly browned.

4. Place chocolate chips and shortening in small microwave-safe bowl. Microwave at MEDIUM (50%) 30 seconds; stir. If necessary, microwave at MEDIUM an additional 10 seconds at a time, stirring after each heating, just until chips are melted when stirred. Drizzle evenly over top of baked mixture. Cool completely. Cut into bars.

Awesome Cookies

Chocolate Dipped Toffee Bits Cookies

Makes 4 dozen cookies

- 2¼ **cups all-purpose flour**
- 1 **teaspoon baking soda**
- ½ **teaspoon salt**
- ½ **cup (1 stick) butter or margarine, softened**
- ¾ **cup granulated sugar**
- ¾ **cup packed light brown sugar**
- 1 **teaspoon vanilla extract**
- 2 **eggs**
- 1⅓ **cups (8-ounce package) HEATH BITS 'O BRICKLE Toffee Bits**
- 1¾ **cups (10-ounce package) HERSHEY'S MINI KISSES**BRAND **Milk Chocolates**
- 2 **tablespoons shortening (do not use butter, margarine, spread or oil)**

1. Heat oven to 350°F. Lightly grease cookie sheet or line with parchment paper.

2. Stir together flour, baking soda and salt; set aside. Beat butter, granulated sugar, brown sugar and vanilla in large bowl until well blended. Add eggs; beat well. Gradually add flour mixture, beating until well blended. Stir in toffee bits. Drop by rounded teaspoons onto prepared cookie sheet.

3. Bake 9 to 11 minutes or until lightly browned. Cool slightly; remove from cookie sheet to wire rack. Cool completely.

4. Line tray with wax paper. Place chocolates and shortening in medium, microwave-safe bowl. Microwave at MEDIUM (50%) 1 minute; stir. If necessary, microwave at MEDIUM an additional 15 seconds at a time, stirring after each heating, until chocolates are melted and mixture is smooth when stirred.

5. Dip about one-half of each cookie into melted chocolate. Shake gently and scrape cookie bottom on edge of bowl to remove excess chocolate. Place on prepared tray. Refrigerate until chocolate is firm, about 30 minutes. Store in cool, dry place with wax paper between layers of cookies.

White Chocolate Surprise Cookies

Makes about 3½ dozen cookies

⅔ **cup butter or margarine, softened**

1 **cup sugar**

1 **egg**

1 **tablespoon milk**

½ **teaspoon vanilla extract**

1½ **cups all-purpose flour**

⅓ **cup HERSHEY'S SPECIAL DARK Cocoa or HERSHEY'S Cocoa**

½ **teaspoon baking soda**

¼ **teaspoon salt**

About 54 HERSHEY'S BLISS White Chocolates with Meltaway Center, divided

1. Beat butter and sugar in large mixing bowl; add egg, milk and vanilla, blending thoroughly. Stir together flour, cocoa, baking soda and salt. Add to butter mixture, blending well. Refrigerate dough about 1 hour or until firm enough to handle. (Dough will be a little soft.)

2. Heat oven to 350°F. Lightly grease cookie sheet or line with parchment paper. Remove wrappers from white chocolates.

3. Roll dough into 1-inch balls. For each cookie, flatten ball slightly; press chocolate piece into dough. Mold dough around chocolate so that it is completely covered. Place on prepared cookie sheet.

4. Bake 10 to 12 minutes or until cookie is set. Cool slightly; remove from cookie sheet to wire rack. Cool completely.

5. Chop remaining chocolates; place in small microwave-safe bowl. Microwave at MEDIUM (50%) 30 seconds; stir. If necessary, microwave at MEDIUM an additional 10 seconds at a time, stirring after each heating, until chocolate is melted when stirred. Drizzle over tops of cookies; allow to set.

Almond Shortbread Cookies with Chocolate Filling

Makes about 44 sandwich cookies

¾ **cup sliced almonds, toasted***

1 **cup (2 sticks) butter or margarine, softened**

¾ **cup granulated sugar**

3 **egg yolks**

¾ **teaspoon almond extract**

2 **cups all-purpose flour**

CHOCOLATE FILLING (recipe follows)

Powdered sugar (optional)

1. Finely chop almonds; set aside.

2. Beat butter and granulated sugar in large bowl until creamy. Add egg yolks and almond extract; beat well. Gradually add flour, beating until well blended. Stir in almonds. Refrigerate dough 1 to 2 hours or until firm enough to handle.

3. Heat oven to 350°F. On well-floured surface, roll about ¼ of dough to about ⅛-inch thickness (keep remaining dough in refrigerator). Using 2-inch round cookie cutter, cut into equal number of rounds. Place on ungreased cookie sheet. Repeat with remaining dough.

4. Bake 8 to 10 minutes or until almost set. Cool slightly; remove from cookie sheet to wire rack. Cool completely. Spread about 1 measuring teaspoonful CHOCOLATE FILLING onto bottom of one cookie. Top with remaining cookies; gently press together. Repeat with second cookie; spread set, about 1 hour. Lightly sift powdered sugar over top of cookies, if desired. Cover; store at room temperature.

Chocolate Filling: Combine 1 cup HERSHEY'S Milk Chocolate Chips** and ⅓ cup whipping cream in small saucepan. Stir constantly over low heat until mixture is smooth. Remove from heat. Cool about 20 minutes or until slightly thickened and spreadable. Makes about 1 cup filling.

*To toast almonds: Heat oven to 350°F. Spread almonds in thin layer in shallow baking pan. Bake 8 to 10 minutes, stirring occasionally, until light golden brown; cool.

**HERSHEY'S SPECIAL DARK Chocolate Chips or HERSHEY'S Semi-Sweet Chocolate Chips may also be used.

Peanut Butter Cup Brownie Drops

Makes about 4 dozen cookies

38 to 40 REESE'S Peanut Butter Cups Miniatures
¾ cup (1½ sticks) butter or margarine
1½ cups sugar
¾ cup HERSHEY'S Cocoa
2 eggs
2 teaspoons vanilla extract
1 cup all-purpose flour
½ teaspoon salt
¼ teaspoon baking soda

1. Heat oven to 350°F. Line cookie sheets with parchment paper or lightly grease. Remove wrappers from peanut butter cups. Cut each peanut butter cup into 4 pieces; set aside.

2. Melt butter in medium saucepan over low heat. Add sugar and cocoa; stir to blend. Remove from heat; stir in eggs and vanilla. Stir together flour, salt and baking soda; stir into chocolate mixture. Stir in peanut butter cup pieces.*

3. Drop by heaping teaspoons onto prepared cookie sheets. Bake 10 to 12 minutes or until set and edges are firm. Do not overbake. Cool slightly; remove from cookie sheet to wire rack. Cool completely.

For more visible peanut butter cup pieces, some of the pieces can be held back and then pushed into the cookies just as they come out of the oven.

Lemon Coconut Pixies

Makes about 4 dozen cookies

¼ cup (½ stick) butter or margarine, softened

1 cup granulated sugar

2 eggs

1½ teaspoons freshly grated lemon peel

1½ cups all-purpose flour

2 teaspoons baking powder

¼ teaspoon salt

1 cup MOUNDS Sweetened Coconut Flakes

Powdered sugar

1. Beat butter, granulated sugar, eggs and lemon peel in large bowl until well blended. Stir together flour, baking powder and salt; gradually add to lemon mixture, beating until blended. Stir in coconut. Cover; refrigerate dough about 1 hour or until firm enough to handle.

2. Heat oven to 300°F. Line cookie sheets with parchment paper or lightly grease. Shape into 1-inch balls; roll in powdered sugar. Place 2 inches apart on prepared cookie sheet.

3. Bake 15 to 18 minutes or until edges are set. Slide parchment paper and cookies to wire rack or remove cookies from greased cookie sheet to wire rack. Cool completely. Store in tightly covered container in cool, dry place.

Double Striped
Peanut Butter Oatmeal Cookies

Makes about 4 dozen cookies

¾ **cup REESE'S Creamy Peanut Butter**

½ **cup (1 stick) butter or margarine, softened**

⅓ **cup granulated sugar**

⅓ **cup packed light brown sugar**

1 **egg**

2 **tablespoons milk**

1 **teaspoon vanilla extract**

1⅓ **cups quick-cooking oats, divided**

1 **cup all-purpose flour**

1 **teaspoon baking soda**

½ **teaspoon salt**

½ **cup HERSHEY'S Milk Chocolate Chips**

2 **teaspoons shortening (do not use butter, margarine, spread or oil), divided**

½ **cup REESE'S Peanut Butter Chips**

1. Heat oven to 350°F. Beat peanut butter and butter in large bowl until well blended. Add granulated sugar and brown sugar; beat until fluffy. Add egg, milk and vanilla; beat well. Stir together ½ cup oats, flour, baking soda and salt; gradually beat into peanut butter mixture.

2. Shape dough into 1-inch balls. Roll in remaining oats; place on ungreased cookie sheet. Flatten cookies with tines of fork to form a crisscross pattern.

3. Bake 10 to 12 minutes or until lightly browned. Cool slightly; remove from cookie sheet to wire rack. Cool completely.

4. Place chocolate chips and 1 teaspoon shortening in medium microwave-safe container. Microwave at MEDIUM (50%) 30 seconds; stir. If necessary, microwave at MEDIUM an additional 10 seconds at a time, stirring after each heating, until chocolate is melted and smooth when stirred. Drizzle over cookies. Repeat procedure with peanut butter chips and remaining 1 teaspoon shortening. Allow drizzles to set.

Toffee Studded Snickerdoodles

Makes about 5 dozen cookies

½ cup (1 stick) butter or margarine, softened
½ cup shortening
1⅓ cups sugar, divided
2 eggs
2¾ cups all-purpose flour
2 teaspoons cream of tartar
1 teaspoon baking soda
¼ teaspoon salt
1⅓ cups (8-ounce package) HEATH BITS 'O BRICKLE Toffee Bits
2 teaspoons ground cinnamon

1. Heat oven to 400°F.

2. Beat butter, shortening and 1 cup sugar in large bowl until fluffy. Add eggs; beat thoroughly. Stir together flour, cream of tartar, baking soda and salt; gradually add to butter mixture, beating until well blended. Stir in toffee bits.

3. Stir together remaining ⅓ cup sugar and cinnamon. Shape dough into 1¼-inch balls; roll in sugar-cinnamon mixture. Place on ungreased cookie sheets.

4. Bake 9 to 11 minutes or until lightly browned around edges. Cool 1 minute; remove from cookie sheets to wire racks. Cool completely.

Double Chocolate Coconut Oatmeal Cookies

Makes about 2½ dozen cookies

1 cup shortening

1¾ cups packed light brown sugar

3 eggs

2 teaspoons vanilla extract

1⅓ cups all-purpose flour

½ cup HERSHEY'S Cocoa

2 teaspoons baking soda

¼ teaspoon salt

½ cup water

3 cups rolled oats or quick-cooking oats

2 cups (12-ounce package) HERSHEY'S SPECIAL DARK Chocolate Chips or HERSHEY'S Semi-Sweet Chocolate Chips, divided

2 cups MOUNDS Sweetened Coconut Flakes, divided

1 cup coarsely chopped nuts

1. Beat shortening, brown sugar, eggs and vanilla in large bowl until well blended. Stir together flour, cocoa, baking soda and salt; add alternately with water to shortening mixture. Stir in oats, 1 cup chocolate chips, 1 cup coconut and nuts, blending well. Cover; refrigerate 2 hours.

2. Heat oven to 350°F. Lightly grease cookie sheet or line with parchment paper. Using ¼-cup ice cream scoop or measuring cup, drop dough about 4 inches apart onto prepared cookie sheet. Sprinkle cookie tops with remaining coconut. Top with remaining chocolate chips (about 9 chips per cookie); lightly press into dough.

3. Bake 10 to 12 minutes or until set (do not overbake). Cool slightly; remove from cookie sheet to wire rack. Cool completely.

Oatmeal Butterscotch Cookies

Makes about 4 dozen cookies

¾ cup (1½ sticks) butter or margarine, softened

¾ cup granulated sugar

¾ cup packed light brown sugar

2 eggs

1 teaspoon vanilla extract

1¼ cups all-purpose flour

1 teaspoon baking soda

½ teaspoon ground cinnamon

½ teaspoon salt

3 cups quick-cooking or regular rolled oats, uncooked

1¾ cups (11-ounce package) HERSHEY'S Butterscotch Chips

1. Heat oven to 375°F.

2. Beat butter, granulated sugar and brown sugar in large bowl until well blended. Add eggs and vanilla; beat well.

3. Combine flour, baking soda, cinnamon and salt; gradually add to butter mixture, beating until well blended. Stir in oats and butterscotch chips; mix well. Drop by heaping teaspoons onto ungreased cookie sheet.

4. Bake 8 to 10 minutes or until golden brown. Cool slightly; remove from cookie sheet to wire rack. Cool completely.

Double-Drizzled
Chocolate Shortbread Cookies

Makes about 6 dozen cookies

- 2 cups (4 sticks) butter or margarine, softened
- 1⅓ cups sugar
- 1 teaspoon vanilla extract
- 4 egg yolks
- 4 cups all-purpose flour
- ½ cup HERSHEY'S SPECIAL DARK Cocoa
- 1 teaspoon salt
- 1 cup chopped pecans
- 1 cup HERSHEY'S SPECIAL DARK Chocolate Chips or HERSHEY'S Semi-Sweet Chocolate Chips
- 2 tablespoons shortening (do not use butter, margarine, spread or oil), divided
- 1 cup REESE'S Peanut Butter Chips or HERSHEY'S Premier White Chips

1. Beat butter, sugar and vanilla until well blended. Add egg yolks, one at a time, beating well after each addition. Gradually add flour, cocoa and salt, beating until blended. (Batter is very stiff.)

2. Divide dough in half. Shape each part into 12-inch-long log. Roll each in pecans, pressing firmly to have pecans adhere. Wrap each roll separately in plastic wrap. Refrigerate 6 to 8 hours.

3. Heat oven to 350°F. Using a sharp knife, cut rolls into ⅜-inch slices. Place on ungreased cookie sheet. Bake 10 to 12 minutes or until set. Cool slightly. Remove from cookie sheet to wire rack. Cool completely.

4. Place chocolate chips and 1 tablespoon shortening in small microwave-safe bowl. Microwave at MEDIUM (50%) 1 minute; stir. If necessary, microwave at MEDIUM an additional 15 seconds at a time, stirring after each heating, until chips are melted and smooth when stirred. Drizzle over tops of cookies. Melt peanut butter chips or white chips with remaining 1 tablespoon shortening; drizzle over chocolate. Let stand until drizzles are set.

KISSes Treats

KISSES® Macaroon Cookies

Makes about 4 dozen cookies

⅓ cup butter or margarine, softened

1 package (3 ounces) cream cheese, softened

¾ cup sugar

1 egg yolk

2 teaspoons almond extract

2 teaspoons orange juice

1¼ cups all-purpose flour

2 teaspoons baking powder

¼ teaspoon salt

5 cups MOUNDS Sweetened Coconut Flakes, divided

48 HERSHEY'S KISSESBRAND Milk Chocolates

1. Beat butter, cream cheese and sugar with electric mixer on medium speed in large bowl until well blended. Add egg yolk, almond extract and orange juice; beat well. Stir together flour, baking powder and salt; gradually add to butter mixture. Stir in 3 cups coconut. Cover; refrigerate 1 hour or until firm enough to handle. Meanwhile, remove wrappers from chocolates.

2. Heat oven to 350°F.

3. Shape dough into 1-inch balls; roll in remaining 2 cups coconut. Place on ungreased cookie sheet.

4. Bake 10 to 12 minutes or until lightly browned. Remove from oven; immediately press chocolate piece into center of each cookie. Cool 1 minute. Carefully remove to wire rack and cool completely.

Secret KISSES® Cookies

Makes 3 dozen cookies

1 cup (2 sticks) butter or margarine, softened
½ cup granulated sugar
1 teaspoon vanilla extract
1¾ cups all-purpose flour
1 cup finely chopped walnuts or almonds
36 HERSHEY'S KISSES BRAND Milk Chocolates or HERSHEY'S KISSES BRAND Milk Chocolates with Almonds
Powdered sugar

1. Beat butter, granulated sugar and vanilla with electric mixer on medium speed in large bowl until fluffy. Add flour and walnuts; beat on low speed of mixer until well blended. Cover; refrigerate 1 to 2 hours or until dough is firm enough to handle.

2. Remove wrappers from chocolates. Heat oven to 375°F. Using about 1 tablespoon dough for each cookie, shape dough around each chocolate; roll in hand to make ball. (Be sure to cover each chocolate piece completely.) Place on ungreased cookie sheet.

3. Bake 10 to 12 minutes or until cookies are set but not browned. Cool slightly; remove to wire rack. While still slightly warm, roll in powdered sugar. Cool completely. Store in tightly covered container. Roll again in powdered sugar just before serving.

Variation: Sift together 1 tablespoon HERSHEY'S Cocoa with ⅓ cup powdered sugar. Roll warm cookies in cocoa mixture.

MINI KISSES® Blondies

Makes 24 bars

½ **cup (1 stick) butter or margarine, softened**
1⅓ **cups packed light brown sugar**
2 **eggs**
2 **teaspoons vanilla extract**
¼ **teaspoon salt**
2 **cups all-purpose flour**
2 **teaspoons baking powder**
1½ **cups (10-ounce package) HERSHEY'S MINI KISSES**BRAND **Milk Chocolates**
1¼
½ **cup chopped nuts**

1. Heat oven to 350°F. Lightly grea[...] baking pan.

2. Beat butter and brown sugar in large b[...] fluffy. Add eggs, vanilla and salt; beat until b[...] Add flour and baking powder; beat just until blended. Stir in chocolate pieces. Spread batter i[...] prepared pan. Sprinkle nuts over top.

3. Bake 28 to 30 minutes or until set and golden brown. Cool completely in pan on wire rack. Cut into bars.

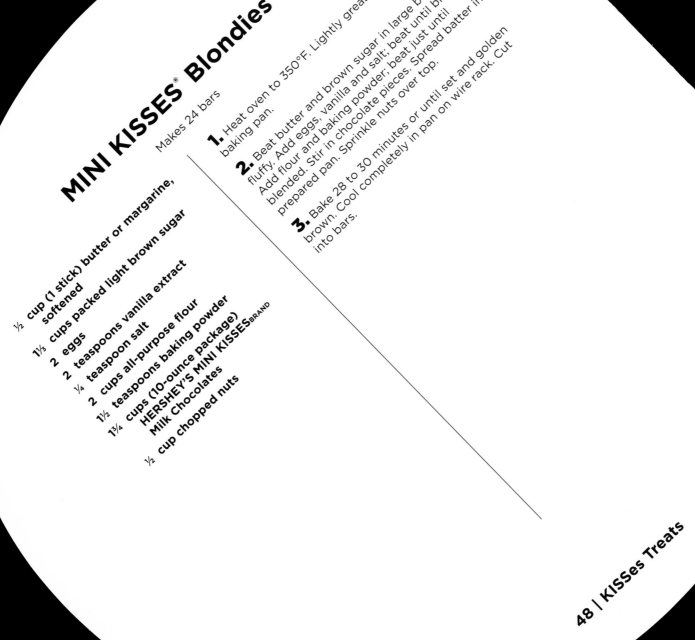

Chocolate Almond Thumbprint Cookies

Makes about 3½ dozen cookies

1 cup (2 sticks) butter or margarine, softened
⅔ cup granulated sugar
2 egg yolks
1 teaspoon vanilla extract
2 cups all-purpose flour
½ cup HERSHEY'S Cocoa
¼ teaspoon salt
½ cup finely chopped almonds
1 cup CHOCOLATE FILLING (recipe follows)
42 HERSHEY'S KISSES BRAND Milk Chocolates with Almonds

1. Heat oven to 350°F. Beat butter, granulated sugar, egg yolks and vanilla until well blended. Stir together flour, cocoa and salt; gradually beat into butter mixture.

2. Roll dough into 1-inch balls; roll balls in almonds. Place on ungreased cookie sheet. Press thumb gently in center of each cookie.

3. Bake 18 to 20 minutes or until set. Remove from cookie sheet to wire rack. Cool completely.

4. Prepare CHOCOLATE FILLING. Remove wrappers from chocolates. Spoon or pipe about ¼ teaspoon filling into each thumbprint. Gently press candy in center of each cookie.

Chocolate Filling: Combine ½ cup powdered sugar, 1 tablespoon HERSHEY'S Cocoa, 1 tablespoon softened butter, 2½ teaspoons milk and ¼ teaspoon vanilla extract in small bowl; beat until smooth.

KISSES® Chocolate Chip Cookies

Makes 4 dozen cookies

48 HERSHEY'S KISSESBRAND Milk Chocolates or HERSHEY'S KISSESBRAND Milk Chocolates with Almonds

1 cup (2 sticks) butter or margarine, softened

⅓ cup granulated sugar

⅓ cup packed light brown sugar

1 teaspoon vanilla extract

2 cups all-purpose flour

1 cup HERSHEY'S Mini Chips Semi-Sweet Chocolate

CHOCOLATE DRIZZLE (recipe follows)

1. Heat oven to 375°F. Remove wrappers from chocolates.

2. Beat butter, granulated sugar, brown sugar and vanilla in large bowl until well blended. Add flour to butter mixture; blend until smooth. Stir in small chocolate chips. Mold scant tablespoon dough around each chocolate, covering completely. Shape into balls; place on ungreased cookie sheet.

3. Bake 10 to 12 minutes or until set. Cool slightly; remove from cookie sheet to wire rack. Cool completely. Prepare CHOCOLATE DRIZZLE; drizzle over each cookie.

Chocolate Drizzle: Place ¼ cup HERSHEY'S Mini Chips Semi-Sweet Chocolate and 1 teaspoon shortening in small microwave-safe bowl. Microwave at MEDIUM (50%) 30 seconds; stir. If necessary, microwave at MEDIUM an additional 10 seconds at a time, stirring after each heating, until chocolate is melted and mixture is smooth when stirred.

HERSHEY'S® Triple Chocolate Cookies

Makes about 4 dozen cookies

48 HERSHEY'S KISSES BRAND Milk Chocolates or HERSHEY'S KISSES BRAND Milk Chocolates with Almonds

½ cup (1 stick) butter or margarine, softened

¾ cup granulated sugar

¾ cup packed light brown sugar

1 teaspoon vanilla extract

2 eggs

1 tablespoon milk

2¼ cups all-purpose flour

⅓ cup HERSHEY'S Cocoa

1 teaspoon baking soda

½ teaspoon salt

1 cup HERSHEY'S SPECIAL DARK Chocolate Chips or HERSHEY'S Semi-Sweet Chocolate Chips

1. Remove wrappers from chocolates. Heat oven to 350°F.

2. Beat butter, granulated sugar, brown sugar and vanilla with electric mixer on medium speed in large bowl until well blended. Add eggs and milk; beat well.

3. Stir together flour, cocoa, baking soda and salt; gradually beat into butter mixture, beating until well blended. Stir in chocolate chips. Shape dough into 1-inch balls. Place on ungreased cookie sheet.

4. Bake 8 to 10 minutes or until set. Do not overbake. Gently press a chocolate in center of each cookie. Remove to wire rack and cool completely.

Variation: For vanilla cookies, omit cocoa and add an additional ⅓ cup all-purpose flour.

HERSHEY'S® HUGS® and KISSES® Candies Chocolate Cake

Makes 12 servings

¾ cup (1½ sticks) butter or margarine, softened

1¾ cups sugar

2 eggs

1 teaspoon vanilla extract

2 cups all-purpose flour

¾ cup HERSHEY'S Cocoa or HERSHEY'S SPECIAL DARK Cocoa

1¼ teaspoons baking soda

½ teaspoon salt

1⅓ cups water

COCOA FUDGE FROSTING (recipe follows)

HERSHEY'S HUGSʙʀᴀɴᴅ Candies or HERSHEY'S KISSESʙʀᴀɴᴅ Milk Chocolates

1. Heat oven to 350°F. Grease and flour 13×9×2-inch baking pan.

2. Beat butter and sugar in large bowl until fluffy. Add eggs and vanilla; beat 1 minute on medium speed of mixer. Stir together flour, cocoa, baking soda and salt; add alternately with water to butter mixture, beating until well blended. Pour batter into prepared pan.

3. Bake 40 to 45 minutes or until wooden pick inserted in center comes out clean. Cool 10 minutes; remove from pan to wire rack. Cool completely. Frost with COCOA FUDGE FROSTING. Remove wrappers from candies; garnish cake as desired with candies.

Cocoa Fudge Frosting

Makes about 2½ cups frosting

- ½ **cup (1 stick) butter or margarine**
- ½ **cup HERSHEY'S Cocoa or HERSHEY'S SPECIAL DARK Cocoa**
- 3⅔ **cups (1 pound) powdered sugar**
- ⅓ **cup milk, heated**
- 1 **teaspoon vanilla extract**

Melt butter in small saucepan over low heat; stir in cocoa. Cook, stirring constantly, until mixture thickens slightly. Remove from heat; pour into small mixer bowl. Add powdered sugar alternately with warm milk, beating to spreading consistency. Stir in vanilla. Spread frosting while warm.

Meltaway Brownie Bites

Makes about 48 brownie bites

48 Any flavor HERSHEY'S KISSESBRAND Chocolates or HERSHEY'S HUGSBRAND Candies

⅔ cup butter or margarine, softened

1¼ cups granulated sugar

1 tablespoon water

1 teaspoon vanilla extract

2 eggs

1½ cups all-purpose flour

½ cup HERSHEY'S Cocoa or HERSHEY'S SPECIAL DARK Cocoa

½ teaspoon salt

¼ teaspoon baking soda

Powdered sugar

1. Remove wrappers from chocolates; place in freezer while preparing and baking cookies.

2. Beat butter, granulated sugar, water and vanilla in large bowl on medium speed of mixer until well blended. Add eggs; beat well. Stir together flour, cocoa, salt and baking soda. Gradually add to sugar mixture, beating on low speed until blended. Cover; refrigerate dough about 2 hours or until firm enough to handle.

3. Heat oven to 350°F. Line 48 small muffin cups (1¾ inches in diameter) with paper or foil baking cups or lightly spray with vegetable cooking spray. Shape dough into 1-inch balls; place in prepared muffin cups.

4. Bake 11 to 13 minutes or until cookie surface is set. Cookies will appear soft and moist. Do not overbake. Cool about 5 minutes on wire rack. Dust cookie tops with powdered sugar. Press frozen chocolate piece into surface of each cookie. Cool completely in pan on wire rack.

Bars & Brownies

Five Layer Bars

Makes about 24 bars

¾ cup (1½ sticks) butter or margarine

1¾ cups graham cracker crumbs

¼ cup HERSHEY'S Cocoa

2 tablespoons sugar

1 can (14 ounces) sweetened condensed milk (not evaporated milk)

1 cup HERSHEY'S SPECIAL DARK Chocolate Chips or HERSHEY'S Semi-Sweet Chocolate Chips

1 cup raisins, chopped dried apricots or miniature marshmallows

1 cup chopped nuts

1. Heat oven to 350°F. Place butter in 13×9×2-inch baking pan. Heat in oven until melted; remove pan from oven.

2. Stir together crumbs, cocoa and sugar; sprinkle evenly over butter. Pour sweetened condensed milk evenly over crumb mixture. Sprinkle with chocolate chips and raisins. Sprinkle nuts on top; press down firmly.

3. Bake 25 to 30 minutes or until lightly browned. Cool completely in pan on wire rack. Cover with foil; let stand at room temperature 6 to 8 hours. Cut into bars.

Golden Bars: Substitute 1 cup REESE'S Peanut Butter Chips for chocolate chips. Sprinkle 1 cup golden raisins or chopped dried apricots over chips. Proceed as above.

English Toffee Bars

Makes about 24 bars

2 cups all-purpose flour

1 cup packed light brown sugar

½ cup (1 stick) cold butter

1 cup pecan halves

TOFFEE TOPPING (recipe follows)

1 cup HERSHEY'S Milk Chocolate Chips

1. Heat oven to 350°F.

2. Combine flour and brown sugar in large bowl. With pastry blender or fork, cut in butter until fine crumbs form (a few large crumbs may remain). Press mixture onto bottom of ungreased 13×9×2-inch baking pan. Sprinkle pecans over crust. Prepare TOFFEE TOPPING; drizzle evenly over pecans and crust.

3. Bake 20 to 22 minutes or until topping is bubbly and golden; remove from oven. Immediately sprinkle milk chocolate chips evenly over top; press gently onto surface. Cool completely in pan on wire rack. Cut into bars.

Toffee Topping: Combine ⅔ cup butter and ⅓ cup packed light brown sugar in small saucepan; cook over medium heat, stirring constantly, until mixture comes to a boil. Continue boiling, stirring constantly, 30 seconds. Use immediately.

Red Velvet Cream Cheese Squares

Makes 24 squares

1 package (16.25 ounces) white cake mix

⅓ cup HERSHEY'S Cocoa

¾ cup sugar, divided

½ cup (1 stick) butter or margarine, melted

2 tablespoons (1-ounce bottle) red food color, divided

1 tablespoon water

3 eggs

1 cup HERSHEY'S SPECIAL DARK Chocolate Chips or HERSHEY'S Semi-Sweet Chocolate Chips

1 package (8 ounces) cream cheese, softened

1 teaspoon vanilla extract

1 container (8 ounces) dairy sour cream

1 tablespoon milk

1. Heat oven to 350°F. Line 13×9×2-inch baking pan with foil, extending foil beyond pan sides. Lightly grease foil.

2. Stir together cake mix, cocoa and ¼ cup sugar; set aside ½ cup cake mixture. Mix remaining cake mixture with melted butter, 1 tablespoon red food color, water and 1 egg until dough forms. Stir in chocolate chips. Press dough evenly on bottom of prepared pan.

3. Beat together cream cheese, remaining ½ cup sugar and vanilla until well blended. Beat in sour cream and remaining 2 eggs. Set aside ½ cup cream cheese mixture; pour remaining mixture in crust, spreading evenly.

4. Beat reserved cake mixture, reserved cream cheese mixture, remaining 1 tablespoon red food color and milk until well blended. Drop by tablespoons onto vanilla batter in pan. Swirl with knife for marbled effect.

5. Bake 30 to 35 minutes or until center is set. Cool completely in pan on wire rack. Cover; refrigerate until chilled. Cut into squares. Refrigerate leftovers.

Chocolate Macaroon Bars

Makes about 24 bars

1¼ cups graham cracker crumbs
⅓ cup sugar
¼ cup HERSHEY'S Cocoa
⅓ cup butter or margarine, melted
1 can (14 ounces) sweetened condensed milk (not evaporated milk)
2⅔ cups MOUNDS Sweetened Coconut Flakes
2 cups fresh white bread crumbs (about 5 slices)
2 eggs
2 teaspoons vanilla extract
1 cup HERSHEY'S Mini Chips Semi-Sweet Chocolate

1. Heat oven to 350°F.

2. Stir together graham cracker crumbs, sugar, cocoa and butter in large bowl; press firmly onto bottom of ungreased 13×9×2-inch baking pan.

3. Bake 10 minutes. Meanwhile, combine sweetened condensed milk, coconut, bread crumbs, eggs, vanilla and small chocolate chips in large bowl; stir until blended. Spoon over prepared crust, spreading evenly.

4. Bake 30 minutes or until lightly browned. Cool completely in pan on wire rack. Cut into bars. Store covered in refrigerator.

Three Layer Cheesecake Squares

Makes 16 servings

CHOCOLATE CRUMB CRUST
(recipe follows)

3 packages (8 ounces each) cream cheese, softened

¾ cup sugar

3 eggs

⅓ cup dairy sour cream

3 tablespoons all-purpose flour

1 teaspoon vanilla extract

1 cup REESE'S Peanut Butter Chips, melted

1 cup HERSHEY'S SPECIAL DARK Chocolate Chips or HERSHEY'S Semi-Sweet Chocolate Chips, melted

1 cup HERSHEY'S Premier White Chips, melted

THREE LAYER DRIZZLE (recipe follows)

1. Heat oven to 350°F. Line 9-inch square baking pan with foil, extending edges over pan sides; grease lightly. Prepare CHOCOLATE CRUMB CRUST.

2. Beat cream cheese and sugar until smooth. Gradually add eggs, sour cream, flour and vanilla; beat well. Stir 1⅓ cups batter into melted peanut butter chips; pour into prepared crust. Stir 1⅓ cups batter into melted chocolate chips; carefully spoon over peanut butter layer. Stir remaining batter into melted white chips; carefully spoon over chocolate layer.

3. Bake 40 to 45 minutes or until almost set. Cool completely on wire rack.

4. Prepare THREE LAYER DRIZZLE. Drizzle, one flavor at a time, over cheesecake. Refrigerate about 3 hours or until drizzle is firm. Use foil to lift cheesecake out of pan; cut into squares. Garnish as desired. Cover; refrigerate leftover cheesecake.

Chocolate Crumb Crust: Heat oven to 350°F. Combine 1½ cups vanilla wafer crumbs (about 45 wafers, crushed), 6 tablespoons powdered sugar, 6 tablespoons HERSHEY'S Cocoa and 6 tablespoons melted butter or margarine. Press onto bottom of prepared pan. Bake 8 minutes; cool slightly.

Three Layer Drizzle: Melt 1 tablespoon REESE'S Peanut Butter Chips with ½ teaspoon shortening, stirring until chips are melted and mixture is smooth. Repeat with 1 tablespoon HERSHEY'S SPECIAL DARK Chocolate Chips or HERSHEY'S Semi-Sweet Chocolate Chips with ½ teaspoon shortening and 1 tablespoon HERSHEY'S Premier White Chips with ½ teaspoon shortening.

White Chip Lemon Streusel Bars

Makes about 24 bars

1 can (14 ounces) sweetened condensed milk (not evaporated milk)

½ cup lemon juice

1 teaspoon freshly grated lemon peel

2 cups (12-ounce package) HERSHEY'S Premier White Chips, divided

⅔ cup butter or margarine, softened

1 cup packed light brown sugar

1½ cups all-purpose flour

1½ cups regular rolled or quick-cooking oats

¾ cup toasted pecan pieces*

1 teaspoon baking powder

½ teaspoon salt

1 egg

½ teaspoon shortening

To toast pecans: Heat oven to 350°F. Spread pecans in thin layer in shallow baking pan. Bake, stirring occasionally, 7 to 8 minutes or until golden brown; cool.

1. Heat oven to 350°F. Lightly grease 13×9×2-inch baking pan. Combine sweetened condensed milk, lemon juice and lemon peel in medium bowl; set aside. Measure out ¼ cup and ⅓ cup white chips; set aside. Add remaining white chips to lemon mixture.

2. Beat butter and brown sugar with electric mixer on medium speed in large bowl until well blended. Stir together flour, oats, pecans, baking powder and salt; add to butter mixture, blending well. Set aside 1⅔ cups oats mixture. Add egg to remaining oats mixture, blending until crumbly; press onto bottom of prepared pan. Gently spoon lemon mixture on top, spreading evenly. Add reserved ⅓ cup white chips to reserved oats mixture. Sprinkle over lemon layer, pressing down lightly.

3. Bake 20 to 25 minutes or until lightly browned. Cool in pan on wire rack. Place remaining ¼ cup white chips and shortening in small microwave-safe bowl. Microwave at MEDIUM (50%) 30 seconds or until chips are melted and mixture is smooth when stirred. Drizzle over baked bars. Allow drizzle to set; cut into bars.

White Chip Lime Streusel Bars: Make as directed above substituting lime for lemon.

Chocolate Almond Macaroon Bars

Makes about 24 bars

2 cups chocolate wafer cookie crumbs

6 tablespoons butter or margarine, melted

6 tablespoons powdered sugar

1 can (14 ounces) sweetened condensed milk (not evaporated milk)

3¾ cups MOUNDS Sweetened Coconut Flakes

1 cup sliced almonds, toasted* (optional)

1 cup HERSHEY'S SPECIAL DARK Chocolate Chips or HERSHEY'S Semi-Sweet Chocolate Chips

¼ cup whipping cream

½ cup HERSHEY'S Premier White Chips

1. Heat oven to 350°F. Grease 13×9×2-inch baking pan.

2. Combine crumbs, melted butter and powdered sugar in large bowl. Firmly press crumb mixture on bottom of prepared pan. Stir together sweetened condensed milk, coconut and almonds in large bowl, mixing well. Carefully drop mixture by spoonfuls over crust; spread evenly.

3. Bake 20 to 25 minutes or until coconut edges just begin to brown. Cool.

4. Place chocolate chips and whipping cream in medium microwave-safe bowl. Microwave at MEDIUM (50%) 1 minute; stir. If necessary, microwave at MEDIUM an additional 15 seconds at a time, stirring after each heating, until chips are melted and mixture is smooth when stirred. Cool until slightly thickened; spread over cooled bars. Sprinkle top with white chips. Cover; refrigerate several hours or until thoroughly chilled. Cut into bars. Refrigerate leftovers.

*To toast almonds: Heat oven to 350°F. Spread almonds evenly on shallow baking sheet. Bake 5 to 8 minutes or until lightly browned.

Layered Cookie Bars

Makes 24 bars

¾ cup (1½ sticks) butter or margarine

1¾ cups vanilla wafer crumbs (about 50 wafers, crushed)

6 tablespoons HERSHEY'S Cocoa

¼ cup sugar

1 can (14 ounces) sweetened condensed milk (not evaporated milk)

1 cup HERSHEY'S SPECIAL DARK Chocolate Chips or HERSHEY'S Semi-Sweet Chocolate Chips

¾ cup HEATH BITS 'O BRICKLE Toffee Bits

1 cup chopped walnuts

1. Heat oven to 350°F. Melt butter in 13×9×2-inch baking pan in oven. Combine crumbs, cocoa and sugar; sprinkle over butter.

2. Pour sweetened condensed milk evenly on top of crumbs. Top with chocolate chips and toffee bits, then nuts; press down firmly.

3. Bake 25 to 30 minutes or until lightly browned. Cool completely in pan on wire rack. Chill, if desired. Cut into bars. Store covered at room temperature.

Chocolate Cranberry Bars

Makes about 24 bars

2 cups vanilla wafer crumbs (about 60 wafers, crushed)

½ cup HERSHEY'S Cocoa

3 tablespoons sugar

⅔ cup cold butter, cut into pieces

1 can (14 ounces) sweetened condensed milk (not evaporated milk)

1 cup REESE'S Peanut Butter Chips

1⅓ cups (6-ounce package) sweetened dried cranberries or 1⅓ cups raisins

1 cup coarsely chopped walnuts

1. Heat oven to 350°F.

2. Stir together vanilla wafer crumbs, cocoa and sugar in medium bowl; cut in butter until crumbly. Press mixture evenly on bottom and ½ inch up sides of 13×9×2-inch baking pan. Pour sweetened condensed milk evenly over crumb mixture; sprinkle evenly with peanut butter chips and dried cranberries. Sprinkle nuts on top; press down firmly.

3. Bake 25 to 30 minutes or until lightly browned. Cool completely in pan on wire rack. Cover with foil; let stand several hours before cutting into bars and serving.

Brownies in a Jar

Makes 1 jar mix

1 cup all-purpose flour
½ teaspoon baking powder
¼ teaspoon salt
1½ cups sugar
⅓ cup HERSHEY'S SPECIAL DARK Cocoa
1 cup REESE'S Peanut Butter Chips or HERSHEY'S Premier White Chips
½ cup HERSHEY'S Mini Chips Semi-Sweet Chocolate BAKING INSTRUCTIONS (recipe follows)

1. Stir together flour, baking powder and salt in a small bowl.

2. Layer the ingredients in a clean 1-quart glass canister or jar in the following order (from bottom to top): sugar, cocoa, flour mixture, peanut butter chips and small chocolate chips. Tap jar gently on the counter to settle each layer before adding the next one. Close jar. Attach card with BAKING INSTRUCTIONS.

BAKING INSTRUCTIONS: Heat oven to 350°F. Grease and flour an 8-inch square baking pan. Combine ½ cup (1 stick) melted and cooled butter and 2 slightly beaten eggs in a large bowl. Gently stir in jar contents. Spread in prepared pan. Bake for 35 minutes. Cool in pan. Cut into bars. Makes 16 brownies.

Chocolate Streusel Bars

Makes about 24 bars

1¾ cups all-purpose flour

1 cup sugar

¼ cup HERSHEY'S Cocoa

½ cup (1 stick) butter or margarine

1 egg

1 can (14 ounces) sweetened condensed milk (not evaporated milk)

2 cups (12-ounce package) HERSHEY'S SPECIAL DARK Chocolate Chips or HERSHEY'S Semi-Sweet Chocolate Chips, divided

1 cup coarsely chopped nuts

1. Heat oven to 350°F. Grease 13×9×2-inch baking pan.

2. Stir together flour, sugar and cocoa in large bowl. Cut in butter until mixture resembles coarse crumbs. Add egg; mix well. Set aside 1½ cups mixture. Press remaining mixture onto bottom of prepared pan. Bake crust 10 minutes.

3. Meanwhile, place sweetened condensed milk and 1 cup chocolate chips in medium microwave-safe bowl; stir. Microwave at MEDIUM (50%) 1 to 1½ minutes or until chips are melted and mixture is smooth when stirred; pour over crust. Add nuts and remaining chips to reserved crumb mixture. Sprinkle over top.

4. Bake an additional 25 to 30 minutes or until center is almost set. Cool completely in pan on wire rack. Cut into bars.

Peanut Butter Fudge Brownie Bars

Makes about 24 bars

1 cup (2 sticks) butter or margarine, melted

1½ cups sugar

2 eggs

1 teaspoon vanilla extract

1¼ cups all-purpose flour

⅔ cup HERSHEY'S Cocoa

¼ cup milk

1¼ cups chopped pecans or walnuts, divided

½ cup (1 stick) butter or margarine

1⅔ cups (10-ounce package) REESE'S Peanut Butter Chips

1 can (14 ounces) sweetened condensed milk (not evaporated milk)

¼ cup HERSHEY'S SPECIAL DARK Chocolate Chips or HERSHEY'S Semi-Sweet Chocolate Chips

1. Heat oven to 350°F. Grease 13×9×2-inch baking pan.

2. Beat melted butter, sugar, eggs and vanilla in large bowl with electric mixer on medium speed until well blended. Add flour, cocoa and milk; beat until blended. Stir in 1 cup nuts. Spread in prepared pan.

3. Bake 25 to 30 minutes or just until edges begin to pull away from sides of pan. Cool completely in pan on wire rack.

4. Melt ½ cup butter and peanut butter chips in medium saucepan over low heat, stirring constantly. Add sweetened condensed milk, stirring until smooth; pour over baked layer.

5. Place chocolate chips in small microwave-safe bowl. Microwave at MEDIUM (50%) 45 seconds or just until chips are melted when stirred. Drizzle bars with melted chocolate; sprinkle with remaining ¼ cup nuts. Refrigerate 1 hour or until firm. Cut into bars. Cover; refrigerate leftover bars.

Fun for Kids

Ice Cream Sandwiches

Makes about 12 (4-inch) ice cream sandwiches

½ cup shortening

1 cup sugar

1 egg

1 teaspoon vanilla extract

1⅔ cups all-purpose flour

⅓ cup HERSHEY'S Cocoa

½ teaspoon baking soda

½ teaspoon salt

¼ cup milk

Desired flavor ice cream, slightly softened

Assorted chopped HERSHEY'S, REESE'S or HEATH baking pieces, crushed peppermints or other small candies (optional)

1. Beat shortening, sugar, egg and vanilla in large bowl until well blended. Stir together flour, cocoa, baking soda and salt; add alternately with milk to sugar mixture, beating until well blended. Cover; refrigerate about 1 hour.

2. Heat oven to 375°F. Drop batter by heaping tablespoons onto ungreased cookie sheet. With palm of hand or bottom of glass, flatten each cookie into 2¾-inch circle, about ¼ inch thick. Bake 8 to 10 minutes or until almost set. Cool 1 minute; remove from cookie sheet to wire rack. Cool completely.

3. Place scoop of ice cream on flat side of 1 cookie; spread evenly with spatula. Top with another cookie, pressing together lightly; repeat with remaining cookies. Roll ice cream edges in chopped baking pieces or candies, if desired. Wrap individually in foil; freeze until firm.

Two Great Tastes Pudding Parfaits

Makes 6 servings

1 package (6-serving size) vanilla cook & serve pudding and pie filling mix*

3½ cups milk

1 cup REESE'S Peanut Butter Chips

1 cup HERSHEY'S MINI KISSESBRAND Milk Chocolates

Whipped topping (optional)

Additional HERSHEY'S MINI KISSESBRAND Milk Chocolates or grated chocolate

*Do not use instant pudding mix.

1. Combine pudding mix and 3½ cups milk in large heavy saucepan (rather than amount listed in package directions). Cook over medium heat, stirring constantly, until mixture comes to a full boil. Remove from heat; divide hot mixture between 2 heatproof medium bowls.

2. Immediately stir peanut butter chips into mixture in one bowl and chocolates into second bowl. Stir both mixtures until chips are melted and mixture is smooth. Cool slightly, stirring occasionally.

3. Alternately layer peanut butter and chocolate mixtures in parfait dishes, wine glasses or dessert dishes. Place plastic wrap directly onto surface of each dessert; refrigerate about 6 hours. Garnish with whipped topping, if desired, and chocolate pieces.

S'more for Me

Makes 12 desserts

1 package (6-serving size) vanilla cook & serve pudding and pie filling mix*

3 cups milk

8 (1.55 ounces each) HERSHEY'S Milk Chocolate Bars, broken into pieces

12 single-serve graham cracker crumb crusts

1½ cups miniature marshmallows

12 HERSHEY'S MINIATURES Milk Chocolate Bars

Do not use instant pudding mix.

1. Stir together pudding mix and milk in saucepan. Cook over medium heat, stirring constantly, until mixture comes to a full boil; remove from heat.

2. Add chocolate bar pieces; stir until chocolate is melted and mixture is smooth.

3. Spoon about ⅓ cup pudding mixture into each individual graham crust. Press plastic wrap onto pudding surface; refrigerate until ready to serve. (This step may be done up to 3 days before serving.)

To Serve: Heat oven to 350°F. Remove plastic wrap. Place 10 to 12 miniature marshmallows on surface of each pudding. Bake 10 minutes or until marshmallows are puffed and lightly toasted. Place on serving plate; gently place unwrapped miniature chocolate bar on top of marshmallows. Serve immediately.**

**Dessert will be hot, but should cool sufficiently by the time it gets to the table. Pudding will be warm and the chocolate bar will be slightly melted.

Drizzled Party Popcorn

Makes about 8 cups popcorn

8 cups popped popcorn

½ cup HERSHEY'S Milk Chocolate Chips

2 teaspoons shortening (do not use butter, margarine, spread or oil), divided

½ cup REESE'S Peanut Butter Chips

1. Line cookie sheet or jelly-roll pan with wax paper. Spread popcorn in thin layer on prepared pan.

2. Place milk chocolate chips and 1 teaspoon shortening in microwave-safe bowl. Microwave at MEDIUM (50%) 30 seconds; stir. If necessary, microwave at MEDIUM an additional 10 seconds at a time, stirring after each heating, until chips are melted and smooth when stirred. Drizzle over popcorn.

3. Place peanut butter chips and remaining 1 teaspoon shortening in separate microwave-safe bowl. Microwave at MEDIUM 30 seconds; stir. If necessary, microwave at MEDIUM an additional 10 seconds at a time, stirring after each heating, until chips are melted and smooth when stirred. Drizzle over popcorn.

4. Allow drizzle to set up at room temperature or refrigerate about 10 minutes or until firm. Break popcorn into pieces.

Notes: Popcorn is best eaten the same day as prepared, but it can be stored in an airtight container. Recipe amounts can be changed to match your personal preferences.

Cut Out Chocolate Cookies

Makes about 3 dozen cookies

½ **cup (1 stick) butter or margarine, softened**
¾ **cup sugar**
1 **egg**
1 **teaspoon vanilla extract**
1½ **cups all-purpose flour**
⅓ **cup HERSHEY'S Cocoa**
½ **teaspoon baking powder**
½ **teaspoon baking soda**
¼ **teaspoon salt**
VANILLA GLAZE (recipe follows)

1. Beat butter, sugar, egg and vanilla in large bowl until fluffy. Combine flour, cocoa, baking powder, baking soda and salt; add to butter mixture, blending well. Chill dough about 1 hour or until firm enough to roll.

2. Heat oven to 325°F.

3. On lightly floured board or between 2 pieces of wax paper, roll small portion of dough at a time to ¼-inch thickness. Cut into desired shapes with cookie cutters; place on ungreased cookie sheet.

4. Bake 5 to 7 minutes or until no indentation remains when touched lightly. Cool slightly; remove from cookie sheet to wire racks. Cool completely. Frost with VANILLA GLAZE. Decorate as desired.

Vanilla Glaze

Makes about ¾ cup glaze

Melt butter in small saucepan over low heat. Remove from heat; blend in powdered sugar and vanilla. Add milk gradually, beating with spoon or wire whisk until glaze is of desired consistency. Blend in food color, if desired.

3 tablespoons butter or margarine
2 cups powdered sugar
1 teaspoon vanilla extract
2 to 3 tablespoons milk
2 to 4 drops food color (optional)

Peanut Butter Cup Pinwheels

Makes about 36 cookies

1 package (8 ounces) cream cheese, softened
1 cup (2 sticks) butter or margarine, softened
¼ cup granulated sugar
1 teaspoon vanilla extract
2¼ cups all-purpose flour
⅛ teaspoon salt
36 to 40 REESE'S Peanut Butter Cups Miniatures
Additional granulated sugar
Powdered sugar
3 tablespoons REESE'S Creamy Peanut Butter

1. Beat cream cheese, butter, ¼ cup granulated sugar and vanilla in large mixer bowl until light and fluffy. Stir together flour and salt; gradually beat into cream cheese mixture, beating until well blended. Divide dough into half; cover and refrigerate about an hour or until firm.

2. Remove wrappers from peanut butter cups. Carefully place each peanut butter cup on its side and cut through the cup, separating the top from the peanut butter filling and bottom. Set the peanut butter cup tops aside. Chop the bottom sections with a little bit of granulated sugar into very fine pieces; set aside. (The granulated sugar helps to keep the mixture from clumping.)

3. Heat oven to 350°F. Line cookie sheets with parchment paper or grease lightly. Roll half of dough at a time on lightly floured surface to a thickness of ⅛ inch. (Keep remaining dough in refrigerator until ready to use.) Cut into 3-inch squares. Use spatula to lift and place squares 1 inch apart on prepared cookie sheets.

4. Place about 1 teaspoon of chopped peanut butter cup mixture in center of each square. Cut from each corner of square to within ½ inch of center and filling. Bring every other point into center and press dough together to form pinwheel.

5. Bake 12 to 14 minutes or until lightly browned. Cool cookies completely. Sprinkle cookies with powdered sugar. "Glue" peanut butter cup top to cookie with about ¼ teaspoon peanut butter to form center of pinwheel.

Greeting Card Cookies

Makes about 12 cookies

½ **cup (1 stick) butter or margarine,**
   softened
¾ **cup sugar**
1 **egg**
1 **teaspoon vanilla extract**
1½ **cups all-purpose flour**
⅓ **cup HERSHEY'S Cocoa**
½ **teaspoon baking powder**
½ **teaspoon baking soda**
¼ **teaspoon salt**
   DECORATIVE FROSTING (recipe
   follows)

1. Beat butter, sugar, egg and vanilla in large bowl until fluffy. Stir together flour, cocoa, baking powder, baking soda and salt; add to butter mixture, blending well. Refrigerate about 1 hour or until firm enough to roll. Cut cardboard rectangle for pattern, 2½X4 inches; wrap in plastic wrap.

2. Heat oven to 350°F. Lightly grease cookie sheet or line with parchment paper. On lightly floured board or between two pieces of wax paper, roll out half of dough to ¼-inch thickness. For each cookie, place pattern on dough; cut through dough around pattern with sharp paring knife. (Save dough trimmings and reroll for remaining cookies.) Carefully place cutouts on prepared cookie sheet.

3. Bake 8 to 10 minutes or until set. Cool 1 minute on cookie sheet. (If cookies have lost their shape, trim irregular edges while cookies are still hot.) Carefully transfer to wire rack. Repeat procedure with remaining dough.

4. Prepare DECORATIVE FROSTING; spoon into pastry bag fitted with decorating tip. Pipe names or greetings onto cookies; decorate as desired.

Decorative Frosting

3 cups powdered sugar
⅓ cup shortening
2 to 3 tablespoons milk
 Food color (optional)

Beat powdered sugar and shortening in small bowl; gradually add milk, beating until smooth and slightly thickened. Cover until ready to use. If desired, divide frosting into two or more bowls; tint each a different color with food color.

Chocolate Swirl Lollipop Cookies

Makes about 2 dozen cookies

½ cup (1 stick) butter or margarine, softened

1 cup sugar

2 eggs

1 teaspoon orange extract

1 teaspoon vanilla extract

2¼ cups all-purpose flour, divided

½ teaspoon baking soda

½ teaspoon salt

¼ teaspoon freshly grated orange peel

Few drops red and yellow food color (optional)

2 sections (½ ounce each) HERSHEY'S Unsweetened Chocolate Baking Bar

About 24 wooden ice cream sticks

1. Beat butter and sugar in large bowl until blended. Add eggs and extracts; beat until light and fluffy. Gradually add 1¼ cups flour, blending until smooth. Stir in remaining 1 cup flour, baking soda and salt until mixture is well blended.

2. Place half of batter in medium bowl; stir in orange peel. Stir in food color, if desired. Melt chocolate as directed on package; stir into remaining half of batter. Cover; refrigerate both mixtures until firm enough to roll.

3. With rolling pin or fingers, between 2 pieces of wax paper, roll chocolate and orange mixtures each into 10×8-inch rectangle. Remove wax paper; place orange mixture on top of chocolate. Starting on longest side, roll up doughs tightly, forming into 12-inch roll; wrap in plastic wrap. Refrigerate until firm.

4. Heat oven to 350°F. Remove plastic wrap from roll; cut into ½-inch-wide slices. Place on cookie sheet at least 3 inches apart. Insert wooden stick into each cookie.

5. Bake 8 to 10 minutes or until cookie is almost set. Cool slightly; remove from cookie sheet to wire rack. Cool completely. Decorate and tie with ribbon, if desired.

Cheery Chocolate Animal Cookies

Makes about 4 dozen cookies

1⅔ cups (10-ounce package) REESE'S Peanut Butter Chips

1 cup HERSHEY'S SPECIAL DARK Chocolate Chips or HERSHEY'S Semi-Sweet Chocolate Chips

2 tablespoons shortening (do not use butter, margarine, spread or oil)

1 package (20 ounces) chocolate sandwich cookies

1 package (11 ounces) animal crackers

1. Line trays or cookie sheets with wax paper.

2. Combine peanut butter chips, chocolate chips and shortening in 2-quart glass measuring cup with handle. Microwave at MEDIUM (50%) 1½ to 2 minutes or until chips are melted and mixture is smooth when stirred. Using fork, dip each cookie into melted chip mixture; gently tap fork on side of cup to remove excess chocolate.

3. Place coated cookies on prepared trays; top each cookie with an animal cracker. Chill until chocolate is set, about 30 minutes. Store in airtight container in a cool, dry place.

Chocolate-Peanut Butter Checkerboards

Makes about 4½ dozen cookies

½ cup (1 stick) butter or margarine, softened

1 cup sugar

1 egg

1 teaspoon vanilla extract

1 cup plus 3 tablespoons all-purpose flour, divided

½ teaspoon baking soda

¼ cup HERSHEY'S Cocoa

½ cup REESE'S Peanut Butter Chips, melted

1. Beat butter, sugar, egg and vanilla in large bowl until fluffy. Add 1 cup flour and baking soda; beat until blended. Remove ¾ cup batter to small bowl; set aside. Add cocoa and remaining 3 tablespoons flour to remaining batter in large bowl; blend well.

2. Place peanut butter chips in small microwave-safe bowl. Microwave at MEDIUM (50%) 30 seconds or until melted and smooth when stirred. Immediately add to batter in small bowl, stirring until smooth. Divide chocolate dough into four equal parts. Roll each part between plastic wrap or wax paper into log 7 inches long and about 1 inch in diameter. Repeat with peanut butter dough. Wrap each roll individually in wax paper or plastic wrap. Refrigerate several hours until very firm.

3. Heat oven to 350°F. Remove rolls from wax paper. Place 1 chocolate roll and 1 peanut butter roll side by side on cutting board. Top each roll with another roll of opposite flavor to make checkerboard pattern. Lightly press rolls together; repeat with remaining four rolls. Working with one checkerboard at a time (keep remaining checkerboard covered and refrigerated), cut into ¼-inch slices. Place on ungreased cookie sheet.

4. Bake 8 to 9 minutes or until peanut butter portion is lightly browned. Cool 1 minute; remove from cookie sheet to wire rack. Cool completely.

Peanut Butter and
Milk Chocolate Chip Cattails

Makes 14 coated pretzels

1 cup HERSHEY'S Milk Chocolate Chips, divided

1 cup REESE'S Peanut Butter Chips, divided

2 teaspoons shortening (do not use butter, margarine, spread or oil)

14 pretzel rods

1. Stir together milk chocolate chips and peanut butter chips. Place sheet of wax paper on tray or counter top. Finely chop 1 cup chip mixture in food processor or by hand; place on wax paper. Line tray or cookie sheet with wax paper.

2. Place remaining 1 cup chip mixture and shortening in narrow deep microwave-safe bowl. Microwave at MEDIUM (50%) 1 minute; stir. If necessary, microwave additional 15 seconds at a time, stirring after each heating, until chips are melted and mixture is smooth when stirred.

3. Spoon chocolate-peanut butter mixture over about ¾ of pretzel rod; gently shake off excess. Holding pretzel by uncoated end, roll in chopped chips, pressing chips into chocolate. Place on prepared tray. Refrigerate 30 minutes or until set. Store coated pretzels in cool, dry place.

Variation: Melt 1 cup milk chocolate chips and 1 cup peanut butter chips with 4 teaspoons shortening; dip small pretzels into mixture.

Holiday Cookies on a Stick

Makes about 18 (3½-inch) cookies

1 cup (2 sticks) butter or margarine, softened

¾ cup granulated sugar

¾ cup packed light brown sugar

1 teaspoon vanilla extract

2 eggs

2⅓ cups all-purpose flour

½ cup HERSHEY'S Cocoa

1 teaspoon baking soda

½ teaspoon salt

   About 18 wooden ice cream sticks

1 container (16 ounces) vanilla ready-to-spread frosting (optional)

   Decorating icing in tube, colored sugar, candy sprinkles, HERSHEY'S MINI KISSESBRAND Milk Chocolates

1. Heat oven to 350°F.

2. Beat butter, granulated sugar, brown sugar and vanilla in large bowl on medium speed of mixer until creamy. Add eggs; beat well. Stir together flour, cocoa, baking soda and salt; gradually add to butter mixture, beating until well blended.

3. Drop dough by scant ¼ cupfuls onto ungreased cookie sheet, about 3 inches apart. Shape into balls. Insert wooden stick about three-fourths of the way into side of each ball. Flatten slightly.

4. Bake 8 to 10 minutes or until set. (Cookies will spread during baking.) Cool 3 minutes; using wide spatula, carefully remove from cookie sheet to wire rack. Cool completely.

5. Spread with frosting, if desired. Decorate as desired with holiday motifs, such as a star, tree, candy cane, holly and Santa using decorating icing and garnishes.

Holidays & Party Time

Jack-O-Lantern Brownie

Makes 10 servings

¾ cup (1½ sticks) butter or margarine, melted

1½ cups sugar

1½ teaspoons vanilla extract

3 eggs

¾ cup all-purpose flour

½ cup HERSHEY'S Cocoa

½ teaspoon baking powder

¼ teaspoon salt

Yellow and red food color

1 can (16 ounces) vanilla frosting

Suggested garnishes: HERSHEY'S MINI KISSES BRAND Milk Chocolates, assorted candies such as TWIZZLERS NIBS Licorice Bits, TWIZZLERS PULL-N-PEEL, HEATH English Toffee Bits

1. Heat oven to 350°F. Grease 12-inch round pizza pan. If using a disposable pan, place on baking sheet to bake.

2. Beat melted butter, sugar and vanilla with spoon in large bowl. Beat in eggs. Stir in dry ingredients; beat with spoon until well blended. Spread in pan.

3. Bake 20 to 22 minutes or until top springs back when touched lightly in center. Cool completely. Add yellow and red food color to frosting for desired shade of orange. Frost brownie; garnish to resemble a Jack-O-Lantern.

Boo Bites

Makes about 4 dozen pieces

¼ cup (½ stick) butter or margarine

30 large marshmallows or 3 cups miniature marshmallows

¼ cup light corn syrup

½ cup REESE'S Creamy Peanut Butter

⅓ cup HERSHEY'S SPECIAL DARK Chocolate Chips or HERSHEY'S Semi-Sweet Chocolate Chips

4½ cups crisp rice cereal

1. Line cookie sheet with wax paper.

2. Melt butter in large saucepan over low heat. Add marshmallows. Cook, stirring constantly, until marshmallows are melted. Remove from heat. Add corn syrup; stir until well blended. Add peanut butter and chocolate chips; stir until chips are melted and mixture is well blended.

3. Add cereal; stir until evenly coated. Cool slightly. With wet hands, shape mixture into 1½-inch balls; place balls on prepared cookie sheet. Cool completely. Store in tightly covered container in cool, dry place.

Holiday Chocolate Shortbread Cookies

Makes about 4½ dozen (2-inch diameter) cookies

1 cup (2 sticks) butter, softened

1¼ cups powdered sugar

1 teaspoon vanilla extract

½ cup HERSHEY'S SPECIAL DARK Cocoa or HERSHEY'S Cocoa

1¾ cups all-purpose flour

2 cups (12-ounce package) HERSHEY'S Premier White Chips

1. Heat oven to 300°F. Beat butter, powdered sugar and vanilla in large bowl until creamy. Add cocoa; beat until well blended. Gradually add flour, stirring until smooth.

2. Roll or pat dough to ¼-inch thickness on lightly floured surface or between 2 pieces of wax paper. Cut into holiday shapes using star, tree, wreath or other cookie cutters. Reroll dough scraps, cutting cookies until all dough is used. Place on ungreased cookie sheet.

3. Bake 15 to 20 minutes or just until firm. Immediately place white chips, flat side down, in decorative designs on warm cookies. Cool slightly; remove from cookie sheet to wire rack. Cool completely. Or, cool cookies completely and decorate as desired. Store in airtight container.

Note: For more even baking, place similar shapes and sizes of cookies on same cookie sheet.

Jingle Bells Chocolate Pretzels

Makes about 24 coated pretzels

1 cup HERSHEY'S SPECIAL DARK Chocolate Chips or HERSHEY'S Semi-Sweet Chocolate Chips

1 cup HERSHEY'S Premier White Chips, divided

1 tablespoon plus ½ teaspoon shortening (do not use butter, margarine, spread or oil), divided

About 24 salted or unsalted pretzels (3×2 inches)

1. Cover tray or cookie sheet with wax paper.

2. Place chocolate chips, ⅔ cup white chips and 1 tablespoon shortening in medium microwave-safe bowl. Microwave at MEDIUM (50%) 1 minute; stir. Microwave at MEDIUM an additional 1 to 2 minutes, stirring every 30 seconds, until chips are melted when stirred.

3. Using fork, dip each pretzel into chocolate mixture; tap fork on side of bowl to remove excess chocolate. Place coated pretzels on prepared tray.

4. Place remaining ⅓ cup white chips and remaining ½ teaspoon shortening in small microwave-safe bowl. Microwave at MEDIUM 15 to 30 seconds or until chips are melted when stirred. Using tines of fork, drizzle chip mixture across pretzels. Refrigerate until coating is set. Store in airtight container in cool, dry place.

White Dipped Pretzels: Cover tray with wax paper. Place 2 cups (12-ounce package) HERSHEY'S Premier White Chips and 2 tablespoons shortening (do not use butter, margarine, spread or oil) in medium microwave-safe bowl. Microwave at MEDIUM 1 to 2 minutes or until chips are melted when stirred. Dip pretzels as directed above. Place ¼ cup HERSHEY'S SPECIAL DARK Chocolate Chips or HERSHEY'S Semi-Sweet Chocolate Chips and ¼ teaspoon shortening (do not use butter, margarine, spread or oil) in small microwave-safe bowl. Microwave at MEDIUM 30 seconds to 1 minute or until chips are melted when stirred. Drizzle melted chocolate across pretzels, using tines of fork. Refrigerate and store as directed above.

Hanukkah Coin Cookies

Makes about 4½ dozen cookies

1 cup (2 sticks) butter or margarine, softened
1 cup sugar
1 egg
1 teaspoon vanilla extract
1¾ cups all-purpose flour
½ cup HERSHEY'S Cocoa
1½ teaspoons baking powder
½ teaspoon salt
BUTTERCREAM FROSTING (recipe follows)

1. Beat butter, sugar, egg and vanilla in large bowl until well blended. Stir together flour, cocoa, baking powder and salt; gradually add to butter mixture, beating until well blended. Divide dough in half; place each half on separate sheet of wax paper.

2. Shape each portion into log, about 7 inches long. Wrap each log in wax paper or plastic wrap. Refrigerate until firm, at least 8 hours.

3. Heat oven to 325°F. Cut logs into ¼-inch-thick slices. Place on ungreased cookie sheet.

4. Bake 8 to 10 minutes or until set. Cool slightly; remove from cookie sheet to wire rack. Cool completely. Prepare BUTTERCREAM FROSTING; spread over tops of cookies.

Buttercream Frosting

Makes about 1 cup frosting

¼ cup (½ stick) butter, softened
1½ cups powdered sugar
 1 to 2 tablespoons milk
½ teaspoon vanilla extract
    Yellow food color

Beat butter until creamy. Gradually add powdered sugar and milk to butter, beating to desired consistency. Stir in vanilla and food color.

Chocolate Cherry Bars

Makes about 24 bars

1 cup (2 sticks) butter or margarine
¾ cup HERSHEY'S Cocoa or HERSHEY'S SPECIAL DARK Cocoa
2 cups sugar
4 eggs
1½ cups plus ⅓ cup all-purpose flour, divided
⅓ cup chopped almonds
1 can (14 ounces) sweetened condensed milk (not evaporated milk)
½ teaspoon almond extract
1 cup HERSHEY'S MINI KISSESBRAND Milk Chocolates
1 cup chopped maraschino cherries, drained

1. Heat oven to 350°F. Generously grease 13×9×2-inch baking pan.

2. Melt butter in large saucepan over low heat; stir in cocoa until smooth. Remove from heat. Add sugar, 3 eggs, 1½ cups flour and almonds; mix well. Pour into prepared pan. Bake 20 minutes.

3. Meanwhile, whisk together remaining 1 egg, remaining ⅓ cup flour, sweetened condensed milk and almond extract. Pour over baked layer; sprinkle chocolate pieces and cherries over top. Return to oven.

4. Bake additional 20 to 25 minutes or until set and edges are golden brown. Cool completely in pan on wire rack. Refrigerate until cold, 6 hours or overnight. Cut into bars. Cover and refrigerate any leftover bars.

Jolly Peanut Butter Gingerbread Cookies

Makes about 6 dozen cookies

1⅔ cups (10-ounce package) REESE'S Peanut Butter Chips

¾ cup (1½ sticks) butter or margarine, softened

1 cup packed light brown sugar

1 cup dark corn syrup

2 eggs

5 cups all-purpose flour

1 teaspoon baking soda

½ teaspoon ground cinnamon

¼ teaspoon ground ginger

¼ teaspoon salt

1. Place peanut butter chips in small microwave-safe bowl. Microwave at MEDIUM (50%) 1 minute; stir. If necessary, microwave at MEDIUM an additional 15 seconds at a time, stirring after each heating, until chips are melted when stirred. Beat melted peanut butter chips and butter in large bowl until well blended. Add brown sugar, corn syrup and eggs; beat until fluffy.

2. Stir together flour, baking soda, cinnamon, ginger and salt. Add half of flour mixture to butter mixture; beat on low speed of mixer until smooth. With wooden spoon, stir in remaining flour mixture until well blended. Divide into thirds; wrap each in plastic wrap. Refrigerate at least 1 hour or until dough is firm enough to roll.

3. Heat oven to 325°F. On lightly floured surface, roll 1 dough portion at a time to ⅛-inch thickness; cut into holiday shapes with floured cookie cutters. Place on ungreased cookie sheet.

4. Bake 10 to 12 minutes or until set and lightly browned. Cool slightly; remove from cookie sheet to wire rack. Cool completely. Frost and decorate as desired.

Sweetheart Layer Bars

Makes 24 bars

1 cup (2 sticks) butter or margarine, divided

1½ cups finely crushed unsalted thin pretzels or pretzel sticks

1 cup HERSHEY'S MINI KISSES BRAND Milk Chocolates

1 can (14 ounces) sweetened condensed milk (not evaporated milk)

¾ cup HERSHEY'S Cocoa

2 cups MOUNDS Sweetened Coconut Flakes, tinted*

*To tint coconut: Place 1 teaspoon water and ½ teaspoon red food color in small bowl; stir in 2 cups coconut flakes. With fork, toss until evenly coated.

1. Heat oven to 350°F.

2. Place ¾ cup butter (1½ sticks) in 13×9×2-inch baking pan; place in oven just until butter melts. Remove from oven. Stir in crushed pretzels; press evenly onto bottom of pan. Sprinkle chocolates over pretzel layer.

3. Place sweetened condensed milk, cocoa and remaining ¼ cup butter (½ stick) in small microwave-safe bowl. Microwave at MEDIUM (50%) 1 to 1½ minutes or until mixture is melted and smooth when stirred; carefully pour over chocolate layer in pan. Top with coconut; press firmly down onto chocolate layer.

4. Bake 25 to 30 minutes or until lightly browned around edges. Cool completely in pan on wire rack. Cut into heart-shaped pieces with cookie cutters or cut into bars.

Easter Nest Cookies

Makes about 3½ dozen cookies

1½ cups all-purpose flour
1 teaspoon baking powder
½ teaspoon salt
¾ cup (1½ sticks) butter
2 cups miniature marshmallows
½ cup sugar
1 egg white
1 teaspoon vanilla extract
½ teaspoon almond extract
3¾ cups MOUNDS Sweetened
Coconut Flakes, divided
JOLLY RANCHER Jelly Beans
HERSHEY's Candy Coated Milk
Chocolate Eggs

1. Heat oven to 375°F.

2. Stir together flour, baking powder and salt; set aside. Place butter and marshmallows in microwave-safe bowl. Microwave at HIGH (100%) 1 to 1½ minutes or just until mixture melts when stirred. Beat sugar, egg white, vanilla and almond extract in separate bowl; add melted butter mixture, beating until light and fluffy. Gradually add flour mixture, beating until blended. Stir in 2 cups coconut.

3. Shape dough into 1-inch balls; roll balls in remaining 1¾ cups coconut, tinting coconut, if desired.* Place balls on ungreased cookie sheet. Press thumb into center of each ball, creating shallow depression.

4. Bake 8 to 10 minutes or just until lightly browned. Place 1 to 3 jelly beans and milk chocolate eggs in center of each cookie. Transfer to wire rack; cool completely.

*To tint coconut: Place ¾ teaspoon water and a few drops food color in small bowl; stir in 1¾ cups coconut. Toss with fork until evenly tinted; cover tightly.

Index

Metric Chart

DIMENSIONS

1/16 inch = 2 mm
1/8 inch = 3 mm
1/4 inch = 6 mm
1/2 inch = 1.5 cm
3/4 inch = 2 cm
1 inch = 2.5 cm

OVEN TEMPERATURES

250°F = 120°C
275°F = 140°C
300°F = 150°C
325°F = 160°C
350°F = 180°C
375°F = 190°C
400°F = 200°C
425°F = 220°C
450°F = 230°C

VOLUME MEASUREMENTS (dry)

1/8 teaspoon = 0.5 mL
1/4 teaspoon = 1 mL
1/2 teaspoon = 2 mL
3/4 teaspoon = 4 mL
1 teaspoon = 5 mL
1 tablespoon = 15 mL
2 tablespoons = 30 mL
1/4 cup = 60 mL
1/3 cup = 75 mL
1/2 cup = 125 mL
2/3 cup = 150 mL
3/4 cup = 175 mL
1 cup = 250 mL
2 cups = 1 pint = 500 mL
3 cups = 750 mL
4 cups = 1 quart = 1 L

VOLUME MEASUREMENTS (fluid)

1 fluid ounce (2 tablespoons) = 30 mL
4 fluid ounces (1/2 cup) = 125 mL
8 fluid ounces (1 cup) = 250 mL
12 fluid ounces (1 1/2 cups) = 375 mL
16 fluid ounces (2 cups) = 500 mL

WEIGHTS (mass)

1/2 ounce = 15 g
1 ounce = 30 g
3 ounces = 90 g
4 ounces = 120 g
8 ounces = 225 g
10 ounces = 285 g
12 ounces = 360 g
16 ounces = 1 pound = 450 g

BAKING PAN SIZES

Utensil	Size in Inches/Quarts	Metric Volume	Size in Centimeters
Baking or Cake Pan (square or rectangular)	8×8×2	2 L	20×20×5
	9×9×2	2.5 L	23×23×5
	12×8×2	3 L	30×20×5
	13×9×2	3.5 L	33×23×5
Loaf Pan	8×4×3	1.5 L	20×10×7
	9×5×3	2 L	23×13×7
Round Layer Cake Pan	8×1½	1.2 L	20×4
	9×1½	1.5 L	23×4
Pie Plate	8×1¼	750 mL	20×3
	9×1¼	1 L	23×3
Baking Dish or Casserole	1 quart	1 L	—
	1½ quarts	1.5 L	—
	2 quarts	2 L	—